THE PREFACE OF THE DIFFICULTY OF THE ART[1]

THANKS be given to God the Creator of all things, who has conducted and renewed us, instructed us, and given us knowledge and understanding. Unless the Lord should keep and guide us, we should be like vagabonds, without guide or teacher; indeed, we would know nothing in this World, unless he taught us himself, who is the beginning, and the knowledge of all things, by his power and goodness over his people. He directs and instructs whom he will, and with mercy leads back into the way of justice. For he has sent his messengers into the darkness, and made plain the ways, and with his mercy replenished such as are attentive. Know Brother, that this our magisterium and honored office of the secret Stone, is the secret of secrets of God, which he has concealed from his people, neither would he reveal it to any, save to those who, like sons, have faithfully deserved it, knowing both his goodness and greatness. For to him who would request the secrets of God, this secret magistery is more necessary than any other. And those wise men who have attained to its knowledge, have concealed part of it, and part they have revealed. For so have I found my wise predecessors agreeing in this point in their worthy books. Whence you shall know that my own disciple, Musa,[2] more honorable in my eyes than all others, has studied many of their books, and labored in the work of the magistery, wherein he has been greatly troubled, and much perplexed by the composition of the same, and likewise being ignorant of the natures of the composition of things. And he has humbly begged at my hands its explanation, and even direction. Yet I would afford him no answer in response thereto, neither would I discern it, but commanded him to read the Books of the Philosophers, and to seek in them that which he craved of me. But he, going his way, read more than a hundred books, as he could find them; namely the true and secret books of noble Philosophers: but in them he could not find that which he desired: Therefore he remained benumbed, and as if out of his mind, though for a year he continually sought it. Whence my disciple Musa, who has deserved to be accounted among the Philosophers in degree and manner of wisdom, has been so doubtful in its composition; and moreover this occurred to him: What shall the ignorant or unlearned do, who do not understand the nature of things, nor is acquainted with their combinations? And when I beheld this in my pre-elect and dearest disciple, moved with pity and compassion toward him, or rather by the divine command and will, I put forth this my book at the approach of my death, wherein I have omitted many things which preceding Philosophers have made mention of in their books. And again I have spoken of some things which they concealed, and would by no means speak of or refer to in their writings. And I have expounded and laid open certain things, which they have hidden under obscure and figurative sayings. And this my Book I have called the *Secrets of Alchemy*: wherein I have named whatsoever is necessary to the investigator of this science or magistery, in a language befitting his sense and understanding. And in this book I have named the four magisteries far greater and better than other wise men have done; of which are Elixir, one mineral, the other animal: but the other remaining two are mineral, and are not the one Elixir, the artifice of which is to wash that which they call bodies; the other of which is to make gold of azoth vive, the making of which is generation, according to the generation or order of generation in the mines, existing in the heart and interior of the earth. And these four magisteries and moreover artifices, the wise have explained in their books of the composition of this magistery. But many fall short of it, and of its operation they have refused to put it in their books; or if one should find it, yet he could not understand it, than which he could find nothing more grievous. And consequently, in this my book, I will declare it and its making. Let him therefore who will read this my book, [first] read some geometry, and in addition learn her measures, that so he may rightly construct his ovens, neither exceeding their mean, either by augmentation or diminution, nor the quantity of the fire. And know also the manner and grade of the vessel of the work. Moreover, let him see and understand what is the most inward root and beginning of the magistery, being to it as the womb is to living creatures, which are engendered in it, and therein take equally their creation and nourishment, as said before. Unless the thing of this magistery find that

4

which is suitable to it, the act and its work shall be destroyed, and its workmen shall not find that which they seek, neither shall the thing itself bring forth into effect generation: for where one cannot find out the cause of generation, or the root and heat itself, it will happen that destruction shall befall the operations. The same will happen in respect of weight, which when it does not agree in the composition, the parts of the same nature, transcending their bounds by augmentation or diminution, the properties of the composition are destroyed with it, and the effect thereof is ruin and moreover void. Whereof I will give you an example: Do you not see that in soap, with which clothes are washed clean and made white, the right composition engenders in it these properties, by reason of equality, and right composition and being duly composed, which participate in length and breadth? Whereupon through this participation they agree, and then appear in it because it was truly made; and thence note that the virtue which before was latent, which they call a property, and is the virtue of washing, is engendered in the composition. But when the quantity[3] of the compound transcends its bounds, either by addition or diminution, the virtue itself passes outside the limits of equality, and becomes contrary, according to the distemperance of the compound. And this you must understand to happen in the composition of our magistery.

CHAP. I.

Of the four Magisteries of the Art,
namely, Solution, Congelation,
Albification, and Rubification

I SHALL now begin to speak of the great artifice which they call Alchemy, wherein I will confirm my sayings, concealing nothing, nor holding back from speaking thereof, save that which is not appropriate to be uttered or named. We say then that in the great artifice there are four magisteries, as the wise have said, namely, to Dissolve, to Congeal, to Whiten and to Redden. And these four quantities are partakers, of which two of them are partakers between themselves, and so likewise are the other two. And either of these double quantities has another quantity partaker, which is the greater quantity partaker after these two. And I mean to say, by these quantities, the quantity of the natures, and weight of the medicines, which are dissolved and congealed in order, wherein neither addition nor diminution enter. But both of these, namely, solution and congelation, shall be in one operation, and make but one work, and that before composition. But after composition, their works shall be diverse. And this solution and congelation, of which we have spoken, are the solution of the body, and the congelation of the spirit, and they are two, yet have one operation. For the spirits are not congealed, except with the solution of the bodies, and likewise the bodies are not dissolved, except with the congelation of the spirit. And when the body and soul are conjoined together, either of them acts in its companion, making it into its likeness. As for example, with water and earth: for when water is conjoined with earth, it strives to dissolve it with its humidity, and its virtue and property, which are in it, making it more subtle than it was before, and rendering it like unto itself: for the water was more subtle than the earth. And thus does the soul work in the body, and after the same manner is the water thickened with the

7

earth, and becomes like unto the earth in density, for the earth is thicker than the water. And know, that between the solution of the body, and congelation of the spirit, there is no difference of time nor diversity of work, as though one should be without the other, even as there is no difference of time between water and earth in the conjunction of their parts, that one might be known or discerned from the other in their operations: but they have one end, and one act, and one and the same operation encompasses within itself both, together, before composition. And I say before composition, lest he that shall read this book, and hear of solution and congelation, as said, should suppose it to be the composition of which the Philosophers speak, for so he should err in his work and knowledge. Because the composition in this artifice or magistery, is a conjunction or marriage of the congealed spirit with the dissolved body, and their conjunction, and their passion, is [made] upon the fire. For heat is its nourishment, and the soul does not forsake the body, neither is it entirely conjoined with it in the conjunction, except by the alteration of both from their virtue and properties, and after the conversion of their natures. And this is the solution and congelation of which the Philosophers have spoken of before. And know that this solution and congelation is now hidden by the wise, by reason of their subtle discourses, with obscure and wholly covered sayings, that so they might alienate the mind of the searcher from its understanding. Whereof you may take this for an example of the sayings of the Philosophers, which in them is covered over and obscure. Anoint the leaf with poison, and you shall verify thereby the beginning of your office, or magistery of the same. And again: Work the solution of the strong bodies with justice, until either of them be converted to its subtility. So likewise in the sayings of the Wise: Unless you convert the bodies into such subtility that they may be impalpable to the touch, you shall not find that which you seek. And if you have not ground them, return back to the operation till they be ground, and made subtle: which you must do, if you would have your desire. And many other such sayings have they of the like. Nor any proof of this fact thus concealed could by any means be attained, until a very plain demonstration thereof was shown and made apparent to him, the former doubt being removed. And likewise they have named that composition, which is after solution and congelation. And afterward they have said, that composition is not complete, except with marriage and putrefaction. And again after these sayings they teach solution and congelation, division, marriage, putrefaction, and composition. And that is because composition is the origin and life of the thing. For unless there were composition, the thing should never be brought about. And division is to separate the parts of the compound, and thus separation has been its conjunction. And I say that the spirit will not dwell within the body, nor be in it, nor by any means remain with it, until the body itself has subtility and tenuousity, as does the spirit. And when it is made tenuous and subtle, and has cast off its density, and its thickness has become thinness, and its grossness and corporeality has become spirituality, then shall it be mingled with the subtle spirits, and imbibed in them, and thus both shall become one and the same, and they shall not be separated, like as water mixed with water. Suppose that of two participating quantities, which are in solution and congelation, the greater is the soul and the lesser is the body: add afterward to the quantity which is the soul, that quantity which is in the body, and it shall participate in the first quantity, but shall participate in virtue only: then work them as we have wrought, and so shall you obtain your desire, and shall verify your line, as saith Euclid. Afterward take its quantity, and note its weight, and add to it as much moisture as it will drink, the weight of which moisture we have not here determined. Then work them with a dissimilar operation, namely imbibing and subliming first; and this operation is that which they call albification, and they call it Yaricht; that is, silver and white lead.[4] And when you have whitened this compound, add to it as much of the spirit as is half of the whole, and set it to working, till it wax red, and then it shall be of the color of alsulfir,[5] which is very red, and the wise have likened it to gold. And the effect hereof leads you to the sayings of Aristotle, who said to his disciple Arda: When the clay is whitened, we call it Yaricht; that is, silver: and when it is reddened, we name it Temeynchum,[6] which is gold. And whiteness is that which tinges copper, and makes it Yharit.[7] And redness is that which tinges Yharit; that is, silver, and makes it Temeynchum; that is, gold. He therefore who is able to dissolve these bodies, to subtiliate, whiten and redden them, and, as I have told you, to compound them by imbibing, and convert them to the same, shall without doubt attain this magistery, and perform the work, of which I have spoken.

CHAP. II.
Of the Things and Instruments necessary
and fit for this Work

AND it behooves you to know the vessels in this magistery, namely

Aludels, which the wise have called cemeteries, or cribbles: because in them the parts are divided and cleansed, and in them the things of the magistery are completed, perfected, and depurated. And every one of these must have an Oven fit for it, and let each of them have a similitude and figure agreeable to the work. Mezleme, and many other Philosophers, have named all these things in their books, teaching the manner and form thereof. And know that in this the wise agree in their sayings, concealing it by signs, and making many books thereof, and instruments which are necessary in these said four things. As for the instruments, they are two in number. One is a cucurbit, with its alembic; the other is an Aludel that is well made. And similarly there are four things necessary to these. And they are bodies, souls, spirits, and waters: and of these four consists the magistery, and the Mineral Work. And they are explained in the books of the wise. Therefore I have omitted them from this my book, and only named in it what the Philosophers did not name. And he who has but little intellect will know which these are. But I have not made this book for the ignorant and unlearned, but composed it rather for the prudent, and those possessing understanding, wisdom, and knowledge.

CHAP. III.
Of the Nature of those Things
pertaining to this Magisterium

KNOW then, that the Philosophers have called them by many names. Whence some have called them mineral,[8] and some animal, but some herbal, and some by the name of natures, for these are natural. Some others have called them by certain names at their pleasure, as seemed good to them. Know also, that their medicines are near to natures, according as the Philosophers have said in their books, that nature draws nigh unto nature, nature is like unto nature, nature is joined to nature, nature is drowned in nature, nature whitens nature, and nature reddens nature; and generation is retained with generation, and generation overcomes with generation.[9]

CHAP. IV.
Of Decoction, and its Effect

AND know, that the Philosophers have named Decoction in their Books. And they have said that they make decoction in things. And this is what engenders them, and changes them from their substances and colors into other substances, and to other colors. And transgress not what I tell you in this Book, but proceed aright. Consider brother, the seed whereon men live, how the heat of the Sun works in it, until the grain goes forth from it, when men and other creatures consume it. Afterward Nature works on it by her heat within man, converting it into his flesh and blood. Evenso is the operation of our magistery. Whence our seed (as the wise have said) is such, that its perfection and progress consists in the fire, which is the cause of its life and death, (which does not grant it life, except with an intermediary,) and its spirituality, which are not mingled but with the fire. Now have I told you the truth, even as I have seen and done it.

CHAP. V.
*Of the Subtiliation, Solution, Coagulation, and Commixtion
of the Stone, and of their Cause and End*

AND know, that unless you subtiliate the body until all become water, it will neither rust nor putrefy, and will not be able to congeal the flitting souls, when the fire touches them: for the fire is that which congeals them by the aid thereof unto them. And similarly the Philosophers have commanded us to dissolve the bodies, and we dissolve them that the heat might adhere to their depths. Afterward we render those bodies dissolved, and congeal them after their solution, with that thing which draws nigh unto it, until we join all those things which have been mingled together by an apt and fit commixtion, which is a just proportion of quantities. Whereupon we conjoin fire with water, and earth with air: and when the thick has been commixed with the subtle, and the subtle with the thick, the one abides with the other, and their natures are converted and made alike, whereas before they were simple; because that part which is generative adds and allots its virtue to the subtle, which is the air: for it adheres to its like, and is a part of the generation. Whence it receives power to move and ascend upward. And cold has power over the thick, because it has lost its heat, and the water has gone out of it, and dryness[10] has appeared upon it. And the moisture has gone out of it by ascending, and the subtle air has mingled itself therewith; for it is its like, and of its nature. And when the thick body has lost its heat and moisture, and cold and dryness have power over it, and they have broken it up into its parts, and have divided it, and there is no moisture to join the divided parts, then the parts withdraw themselves. And afterwards the part which is contrary to cold, since it has continued, and intermingled its heat and its decoction in its parts, which are earth, and having strength or power in them, and having such dominion and conquest over the cold, and driving away the cold, which before was in the thick body, by the victory of heat over it, the parts are converted in its generation, becoming subtle and hot, and striving to dry up with its heat. And afterward the subtle part, which causes natures to ascend, when it has lost its accidental heat, and waxes cold, then [the natures] are converted, and they are thickened, and descend to the center, and then are conjoined the earthy natures, which are subtiliated, and are converted in their generation, and are imbibed in them: and so the moisture conjoins the divided parts. But the earth endeavors to dry up that moisture, encompassing it, and hindering it from departing therefrom: whence that which was hidden appears upon it. Neither can the moisture be separated, but is retained by the dryness. And likewise we see that whatsoever is in the World, is retained by its contrary, or with its contrary; *viz.*, heat with cold, and dryness with moisture. Thus when any one of them abides with its companion, the subtle is mingled with the thick, and these things are made one substance: namely, their hot and humid soul, and their cold and dry body. It then attempts to dissolve and subtiliate with its heat and its moisture, which is its soul, and strives to enclose and retain with its body, which is cold and dry. And thus, by this circuitous route, is its office altered. Now have I declared to you the truth, which I have seen and done, and I admonish you to change natures from their subtility and their substances, with heat and moisture, until they are converted into other substances and other colors.[11] And transgress not what I have set forth in this book, but proceed aright in this magistery, according to your desire.

CHAP. VI.
Of the fixation of the Spirit

AND know, that when the body is commingled with moisture, and is met with the heat of the fire, the moisture is converted upon the body, and dissolves it, and then the spirit cannot issue forth therefrom; because it is imbibed with the fire. And the spirits are fugitive, so long as the bodies are commingled with them, and strive to resist the fire and its flame. And yet these parts can hardly agree, except with a good operation, and continual and long labor: for the nature of the soul is to tend upwards, where the center of the soul is. And who is he who would approve of conjoining two or diverse things, where their centers are diverse, unless it be after the conversion of their natures, and the change of the substance, and the thing, from its nature, which is difficult to find out? Therefore whosoever is able to convert soul into body, and body into soul, and commingle the subtle spirits therewith, shall be able to tinge every body.

CHAP. VII.
Of the Decoction, Contrition, and
Ablution of the Stone

AND know this, that decoction, contrition, cribation and mundification, and ablution with sweet waters, is much needed in this secret and this magistery. Whence he who would take any pains herein, must cleanse the body well, and wash the blackness from it, and the darkness that appears upon it in his operation. And he must subtilitate the body as much as he can, and afterwards mingle therewith the dissolved souls and cleansed spirits, as long as it pleases him.

CHAP. VIII.
Of the Quantity of the Fire, and of its
commodity and discommodity

FURTHERMORE, you must be acquainted with the quantity of the fire, and the commodity of this thing, and also the discommodity, which proceeds from the commodity of the fire. Whereupon Plato, amongst the discourses in his book, saith: "The fire yields commodity or gain to that which is perfect, but discommodity or corruption to that which is corrupt." Thus when its quantity shall be most suitable, it shall prosper, but when it shall be manifold in things, it shall corrupt both beyond measure; namely, the perfect and the corrupt. And for this cause it was requisite that the wise should pour their medicines upon Elixir, to hinder and remove from them the combustion of the fire, and their heat. And Hermes said to his father: I am afraid Father of the enemy in my house. And he answered: Son, take the male Corascene dog, and the bitch of Armenia,[12] join them together, and they shall bring forth a dog of the color of heaven; and imbibe his thirst once in the water of the sea: for he shall keep your friend, and defend you from your enemy, and shall help you wheresoever you become, abiding always with you, both in this world and in the other. Now Hermes meant by the dog and bitch, such things as preserve bodies from the combustion of the fire, and its heat. And these things are waters of calxes and salts, the composition of which is to be found in the books of the wise [who have written][13] of this magistery. And some of the wise have named them sea-waters, and birds' milk, and such like.

CHAP. IX.
Of the Separation of the
Elements of the Stone

THENCE it behooves you, brother, whom God has honored, that you take this honored or precious Stone, which the wise have named, magnified, hidden and concealed, and put it in a cucurbit with its alembic, and separate its natures; that is, the four elements, earth, water, air, and fire. These are body and soul, spirit and tincture. And when you have separated the water from the earth, and the air from the fire, keep both of them by themselves, and take that which descends to the bottom of the vessel, which is the lees, and wash it with a hot fire, until its blackness has been carried away, and its thickness has receded: then whiten it with a good whitening, and make the superfluous moisture to fly away from it, for then it shall be converted, and shall become a white calx, wherein there is no shadowy darkness, nor uncleanness, nor contrariety. Afterward return to the first natures, which ascended from it, and purify them similarly from uncleanness, blackness, and contrariety: and reiterate [these works] upon them so often, until they are subtiliated, purified, and attenuated. And when you have done this, then is thy God merciful. And know brother, that this office is one stone, into which Garib may not enter; that is, anything else. The wise operate with this, and from it proceeds a medicine with which all things may be perfected. Nothing should be commixed therewith, neither in part nor in whole. And this stone is to be found at all times, in every place, and about every man, the search for which should not trouble him who seeks it, wheresoever he be. This stone is vile, black, and fœtid; cannot be bought, is precious, is not light in weight when taken alone; and it is called the Origin of the world; for it rises up like things that germinate. And this is its revelation and appearance to the seekers.

CHAP. X.
Of the Nature of the Stone,
and its Origin

TAKE it therefore, and work it as the Philosopher has said in his book, when he named it thus: Take the stone no-stone, or which is not a stone, neither is it of the nature of stone. Yet it is a stone whose mine is found in the tops of mountains: and by mountains, the Philosopher understands animals. Whereupon he said: Son, go to the mountains of India, and to their caverns, and take from them honored stones, which will liquefy in water when commixed therein. And this water is indeed that which is taken from other mountains and their caverns. They are, Son, stones and are not stones, but we call them so for a similitude which they have to stones. And know that the roots of their mines are in the air, and their heads in the earth, and when they are plucked out of their places, they will be heard, for there will be a great noise. Go with them my son, for they will quickly vanish away.[14]

CHAP. XI.
Of the Commixtion of the separated Elements

AND begin the composition, which is the circuit of the whole work, for there shall be no composition without marriage and putrefaction. The marriage is to commix the subtle with the thick, and putrefaction, is to roast, grind, and moisten until all be commixed together, and made one; so that there should be no diversity in them, nor separation of water mixed with water. And then shall the thick strive to retain the subtle, and the soul shall endeavor to battle with the fire, and endure it. And the spirit shall strive to be drowned in the bodies, and poured out into them. And this must needs be, because the dissolved body, when it is commixed with the soul, it is likewise commixed with it, and with every part thereof: and other things enter into others according to their similitude, and are converted into one and the same thing. And therefore it is necessary that the soul partake of the commodity, durability, and permanency, which the body received in its commixtion. And it is likewise appropriate that the spirit should partake in this state or permanency of the soul and body; for when the spirit shall be commixed with it by laborious operation, and its parts are commixed with all the parts of the other two, which are, namely, the soul and body, then shall the spirit and both of the others, be converted into one indivisible thing, according to their complete substance, the natures of which have been preserved, and their parts have come together; whence it is that when this compound has met with a dissolved body, and the heat has gotten hold of it, and the moisture which was in it appears upon its face, and is liquefied in the dissolved body, and has passed into it, and commixed itself with that which is of the nature of moisture, it is inflamed, and the fire defends itself with it. Whence, when the fire would then dwell with it, it will not suffer the fire to take hold of it; that is, to adhere with an admixture of the spirit and its water. And the fire will not adhere to it until it is pure. And similarly does the water naturally flee from the fire, and when the fire follows it, it would fly away. And thus is the body the cause of the water falling back and being retained, and the water the cause of the oil being retained, that it should not burn nor be consumed. And the oil is the cause of the tincture being retained; and tincture is the cause of making the color to appear, and the cause of showing forth the tincture, wherein there is neither light nor life. This then is the true life and the perfect thing, and the Magistery, and this is what you have sought. Know therefore and understand, and you shall find what you seek, if it please God.

CHAP. XII.
Of the Solution of the compounded Stone

But afterwards, the Philosophers have subtiliated it by dissolving it, that the body and soul might the better be commixed. For all those things which are together in contrition, assation, and rigation, have a certain vicinity and connection one to another, and therefore the fire is able to assume the weaker nature, until it weakens and vanishes away; and similarly it returns upon the stronger parts, until the body remains without the soul. Whence, when they are thus dissolved and congealed, they take up the parts one to another, as well great as small, and from them is made a combination, which is their assumption, and thus these two are converted into one and the same thing. And when this is done, the fire takes from the soul as much as it takes from the body, neither more nor less, and this is the cause of perfection. Whence it is necessary (in the science of Elixir) to afford it a chapter, *viz.*, for expounding the solution of simple bodies and souls. Because bodies do not enter into souls, but rather detain them, and exempt them from all works of sublimation, fixation, retention, commixtion, and their like, except with the first mundification. And know that solution does not transcend these two ways: but indeed it is to extract the interior of things unto their superficies, and this will be solution (an example whereof is that silver is cold and dry in its appearance, but when its interior appears, it is dissolved, for it is then hot and moist); Or the said solution is to acquire to a body an accidental moisture, which it did not before have, and to add to it its own humidity, whereby its parts are dissolved, and this [likewise] will be its solution.

CHAP. XIII.
Of the Coagulation of the dissolved Stone

SOME among the learned have said: Congeal in a bath with a good congelation, as I have told you, and this is the Sulphur—luminous in the darkness, and it is a Red Hyasinth, a fiery and deadly poison, the Elixir which abides upon none; and it is a victorious Lion, a malefactor, a rending Sword, a Tyriac of health, healing every infirmity. And Geber the son of Hayen said: All the operations of this magistery are contained under six things, which are: to put to flight, to melt, to incerate, to make as white as marble, to dissolve, and to congeal. And to put to flight, is to drive away and remove the blackness from the spirit and soul. And to melt is the liquefaction of the body. And to incerate belongs properly to the body and its subtiliation. To whiten, is properly to quickly melt the body. To congeal, is to congeal the body with the prepared soul. Again, to put to flight appertains to the spirit and soul: to melt, whiten, incerate, and dissolve, belongs to the body; and to congeal to the soul. Understand this.

CHAP. XIV.
That there is but one Stone, and of its nature

BAUZAN a Greek Philosopher, when it was demanded of him whether the stone may ever be made of a thing that germinates, saith thus: There are two first stones, viz., the alkali stone, and our stone, which is the life of him who knows it and the making thereof. But him who is ignorant of it, and has not made it, and knows not how it is engendered, or supposing it to be stone, or who does not comprehend whatsoever I have spoken of the means of this stone, [and yet will make a trial of it,] now prepares himself for death, and casts away his money. For unless this honored stone be found, another shall not arise in its place, neither shall natures triumph over it. Its nature is great heat with moderation.

Whence he who knows it, has now learned it [by reading this book], but he that remains ignorant, has lost his labor.[15] It has manifold properties and virtues, for it cleanses bodies of their additions of accidental sicknesses, and preserves sound substances, so that there does not appear, neither is there seen in them the perturbations of contraries, nor the breach of their bond. For this is the soap of bodies, and their spirit, and their soul; which when commixed with them, dissolves them without detriment. This is the life of the dead, and their resurrection, a medicine preserving bodies, and purging superfluities. He who understands, let him understand, and he who is ignorant, let him be ignorant still. For such an office does not arise precious of itself, neither is it involved with selling or buying. Understand its virtue, value, and honor, and then set to work. And a certain wise man has said: "God does not give thee this magistery only for thy audacity, fortitude, and passion, without all the labor. Rather, men labor, and God grants them fortune." Adore therefore God the creator, who would hold out to you so much favor in his said good works.

CHAP. XV.
The manner of Working the Stone at the white

WHEN therefore you would make this honored magistery, take the honored stone, and put it into a cucurbit, enveloping it with an alembic, and closing it well with the lute of wisdom, leaving it to dry. This you shall thus do, however often you will close it with the lute of wisdom, after setting it in very hot dung. Thereafter you will distill it, putting a receiver under it, whereinto the water may distill, and thus you shall leave it, until all the water is distilled, and the moisture dried up, and dryness prevails over it. Afterward you shall take it out dry, reserving the water that is distilled from it, until you have need of it. And you shall take the dry body that remains in the bottom of the cucurbit, and grind it, and put it in the vessel Chalcosolario,[16] the size of which is according to the quantity of the medicine, and bury it in the most exceedingly hot and humid horse-dung you can obtain, the vessel being well shut with the mortar and lute of wisdom, and thus you shall let it remain there. And when you perceive the dung to wax cold, you shall procure other that is most hot, and therein put the said vessel. Thus shalt you do with it forty days, renewing the hot dung as often as there shall be need, and the medicine will dissolve of itself, and become a thick white water: and when you behold it thus, you shall note its

18

weight, and add thereto as much of the water which you kept previously, as will make half its weight, and then close your vessel with the lute of wisdom, and put it again in hot horse-dung; for within it is humidity and heat, and you shall not omit (as we have previously said) to renew the dung, when it begins to cool, until the [term of] forty days is past. For the medicine will then be congealed in the like number of days, as before it was dissolved in. Afterwards take it, and note its entire weight, and according to its quantity take of the water which you made before, grind the body, and subtiliate it, and pour the water upon it. And set it again in hot horse-dung, for a week and a half; to wit, ten days, then take it out, and you shall find that the body has now drunk up the water. Afterward grind it [again], and put thereto of its water, as much as before said. And bury it in dung, and leave it there for another ten days. Afterwards take it out [again], and you shall find that the body has now drunk up the water. Then grind it as before, putting thereto of the aforesaid water, about the aforesaid quantity, and again bury it in the aforesaid dung, and leave it there ten days [longer], and afterward draw it out. And so shalt you do the fourth time also, which when the fourth is completed, you shall draw it forth and grind it; and sublimate it in dung until it is dissolved. Thereupon, take it out, and reiterate it yet once more, for then is its origin perfect, and its work completed. But when this is thus done, and you have brought this thing, O brother, to this honorable state, take two hundred and fifty drams of lead or tin, and melt them. Thereupon, when it is made molten, cast thereon one dram of Cinnabar: that is, of this Medicine, which has been brought to this honorable state and high order, and it shall retain the tin or lead, that it fly not from the fire; and it shall whiten it, and draw from it its dross and blackness, and convert it into a perpetually permanent tincture. Thereupon, take one dram of these two hundred and fifty, and project it upon two hundred and fifty [drammes] of tin or latten, or copper, and it shall convert them into silver, better than that of the mine. And this is the greatest and last work that it can effect, if God wills it.

CHAP. XVI.
The Conversion of the aforesaid Stone into red

AND if you desire to convert this magistery into gold, take of this medicine, which (as said,) you have brought to this honorable state and high order, the weight of one dram, and this according to the manner of your above said example. And put it in the vessel chalcosolario, and bury it in horse-dung for forty days, and it shall be dissolved: afterward you shall give it water of the dissolved body to drink, first as much as is half its weight; afterward, until it is congealed, you shall bury it in most hot dung, as previously said. Then by order you shall proceed in this Chapter of Gold, as you did above in the Chapter of Silver. And it shall be gold, and make gold, God willing. Keep, Son, this most secret Book, and commit it not unto the hands of ignorant men, being the secret of secrets of God: For [by this means] you shall attain your desire, Amen.

HERE ENDS THE SECRETS OF ALCHEMY, WRITTEN IN HEBREW
BY *KALID*, THE SON OF *JAZICH*.

Notes

1. This translation from Latin into English first appeared in the 1597 compilation of treatises entitled *The Mirror of Alchimy*. Another version, which appeared in William Salmon's *Medicina Practica* (1692), while different, appears to have been drawn largely from the 1597 translation. I edited the translation against the Latin version found in Jo. Jacobi Mangeti's *Bibliotheca Chemica Curiosa*, vol. II; pp. 183-9. This treatise was often referred to by later alchemists, and hence is presented, with little commentary, within the *Alchemical Studies Series* as one of its "foundation stones."

2. Fulcanelli interprets *Musa* symbolically: "Musa, the disciple of Calid, is Μυστης, the *initiated*, whereas his master, —our master in everything,— is the heat released by the athanor (lat. *calidus, burning*)." See *Les Demeures Philosophales*, vol. I, ch. VI.

3. The text of the 1597 translation puts *gravity* for *quantity* (Manget puts *quantitas*).

4. *Plumbum album*. In old Latin, this could mean *tin*.

5. William Salmon writes the Arabic word *alsulfir* as *Al-sulfur*, with the annotation *[Cinnabar]*.

6. Pernety, in his *Dictionnaire Mytho-Hermétique*, defines "Temeynchum. Gold of the Philosophers, or their magistery at the red." (A.E. Waite included this in his *Supplement* to the *Lexicon* of Rulandus.)

7. According to the *Dictionnaire Hermétique*, "*Yharit* is the whitening of the latten of the Philosophers, or their silver." However, Calid was listed in the beginning of that Dictionary as one of its sources, and hence the above definition may not be independent. Pernety, in his *Dictionnaire Mytho-Hermétique*, defines "Yharit. The Matter of the work having arrived at the color white, which the Philosophers call their silver." (This was included by A.E. Waite in his *Supplement* to the *Lexicon*

of Rulandus.) Note that Manget has two spellings, *Yaricht* and *Yharit*, whereas the 1597 translation uses only the one.

8. "Mineral"; that is, *of mines*. However, Manget reads *minera*, and the 1597 translation reads *mines*. But the context seems to require *mineral*, and evidently William Salmon would agree.

9. The Author of the *Dictionnaire Hermétique* gives some insight into this ancient and oft-quoted passage:
Nature is joined by Nature, Nature contains Nature, Nature is contained by Nature. The Philosophers speak thus when the black appears, since it is in this conjuncture that the fixed and the volatile, the sulphur and the Mercury are joined together, without ever being separated. *Alt.* This is the Philosophical Mercury, in which is seen the truth of these words: *Nature loves Nature, Nature surmounts Nature, Nature retains Nature.* The reason of it is that the Salt, Sulphur and Mercury which are in the Menstruum of the Philosophers, have the power to dissolve and to extract those which are in the metals, and to be joined amiably and radically with them.

10. Manget, and the 1597 translation, both read: "and *the thing* has appeared upon it." I follow William Salmon here for clarity.

11. The *Dictionnaire Hermétique* gives some additional insight into this passage:
> To Change the Natures: This is to make from the gross or thick the subtle; that is to say, from the body the spirit, and afterwards from the humid the dry; from water earth: and thus one sets what is below above, and what is above below.

12. Pernety, in his *Dictionnaire Mytho-Hermétique*, writes:
> "...Some have given the name of Dog to the matter of the great work. One calls it Dog of Armenia, another says that the Wolf and the Dog are found in this matter; that they have one and the same origin, and nevertheless that the Wolf comes from the East, and the Dog from the West. Rhasis. The one represents the fixed and the other the volatile of the matter. DOG OF ARMENIA is one of the names that the Hermetic Philosophers have given to their sulphur, or to the male sperm of their stone."
> Also: "Bitch of Corascene. Is one of the names that the chymical Philosophers have given to their mercury, or feminine sperm of their stone."

(This was included by A.E. Waite in his Supplement to the Lexicon of Rulandus.) Note that the referenced phrase was quoted in the Rosarium Philosophorum, and later in the Open Entrance... of Philalethes.

13. The bracketed passages are not found in Manget, but did appear in the 1597 translation, and are included for the interpretive clarity no doubt intended by the translator.

14. Surely chapter X is a most peculiar one, yet strangely evocative, and it relates some important alchemical themes. In his *Explication of Calid* (ch. *XXXIV, vs. VII*), William Salmon writes: "In the Mountains of Bodies, in the Plains of Mercury, look for it, there this Water is created, and by concourse of these two, and is called by the Philosophers, their permanent or fixed Water." Yet *Calid* indicates that, by *mountains*, the Philosophers mean *animals!* Concerning the stone *that is no-stone*, Pernety has written *(Dict. Mytho-Herm.)*:

> STONE AND NOT-STONE. The Hermetic Philosophers have given this name to their perfect magistery, and not to the matter from which they make it, as some Chymists inaptly think. They have not called it *stone*, out of any resemblance that it may have to stones, but because, like stones, it resists the attacks of the most violent fire. It is an impalpable powder, most-fixed, heavy and of good odor, whence it has been named powder of projection, and not stone of projection.

Also, concerning *our mines, which have roots in the air...*, Fulcanelli has written (*Le Mystère des Cathédrales*): "...a specific body is needed to serve as a receptacle; an attracting medium, containing a principle capable of receiving the spirit and 'embodying' it. 'Our bodies have roots in the air and heads on the ground' say the Wise..."

Finally, concerning the phrase: "... and when they are plucked out of their places, they will be heard, for there will be a great noise...", this may refer to the mandrake, which was long believed to utter a loud scream when pulled from the earth.

15. Manget actually reads: "Whence he that remains ignorant, has not learned it;" —something of a tautology.

16. *Chalco* — is from the Greek *chalkos,* which means *copper* or *brass.* The Latin word *solarium* can mean "a room exposed to the sun." Whence one may suppose that a *Chalcosolario* is a copper or brass vessel which is open to the sun's rays, and takes its heat therefrom. Both occurrences of "chalcosolario" were omitted from the 1597 translation.

FOR A COMPLETE LIST OF PUBLICATIONS,
PLEASE ADDRESS:
HOLMES PUBLISHING GROUP
POSTAL BOX 623
EDMONDS WA 98020 USA

Alchemical Studies Series 14

First Edition
1st Printing, 1999

ISBN 1-55818-419-8

HOLMES PUBLISHING GROUP LLC
POSTAL BOX 623
EDMONDS WA 98020 USA

The Book of the Secrets of Alchemy

Composed by KALID the son of Jazich, translated out of Hebrew into Arabic, and out of Arabic into Latin, and out of Latin into English. Translator Uncertain.

EDITED BY PATRICK SMITH

The Alchemical Press